SOUTH COAST RAILWAYS ~
BRIGHTON
TO
WORTHING

Vic Mitchell and Keith Smith

MP Middleton Press

Other Middleton Press books featuring aspects of Brighton's history -

BRIGHTON TO EASTBOURNE

BRIGHTON'S TRAMWAYS

THREE BRIDGES TO BRIGHTON

STEAMING THROUGH WEST SUSSEX

WEST SUSSEX RAILWAYS IN THE 1980s

BATTLE OVER SUSSEX 1940

MILITARY DEFENCE OF WEST SUSSEX

Write or telephone for our latest list of local history and transport books

MP Middleton Press

Easebourne Lane, Midhurst, West Sussex, GU29 9AZ
Tel: (0730) 813169   Fax: (0730) 812601

First Published 1983
Reprinted 1983, 1985, 1992
Fourth reprint March 2000

ISBN 0 906520 03 7

© Middleton Press, 1983

Published by
  Middleton Press
  Easebourne Lane
  Midhurst, West Sussex
  GU29 9AZ
Tel: 01730 813169   Fax: 01730 812601

Printed & bound by Biddles Ltd,
  Guildford and Kings Lynn

INDEX

GEOGRAPHICAL SETTING

The coastal plain between the South Downs and the English Channel tapers to a point in the east at Brighton. East of Brighton the Downs outcrop as chalk cliffs. North of the town there is a valley in which the stream is ducted through the urban area in a Victorian brick built culvert, as big as an underground station where it passes under the Steine. The railway terminus was built on the west side of the valley about 100ft. above sea level. This gave an easy route northward but necessitated a 200 yard tunnel for the west coast line and a lengthy curved viaduct to the east.

After descending at 1 in 264 for 5 miles the line to Worthing runs fairly level and almost parallel to the coast. The Horsham branch from Shoreham, however, passes through a gap in the South Downs, a geographical feature of note cut by the River Adur.

ACKNOWLEDGEMENTS

We would like to thank the editor of the Railway Magazine for the use of the map in the introduction and the East Sussex County Library for permission to use photographs from the Madgwick and Wise collections. We would like to record our appreciation of the help received from the photographers named in the captions and also from: R. Archer, J. Barrett, C. R. L. Coles, D. Cullum, C. Durrant, J. Edgington, D. Elleray, R. Good, R. Harmer, J. H. Knight, N. Langridge, C. Packham, D. Osborne, A. Pronger, R. Randell, R. C. Riley, N. Stanyon, Mrs. E. M. Wallis and D. Wallis. Our thanks also go to D. Dornom, M. Grainger, A. G. Richards and H. S. F. Thompson for their darkroom skills. As ever our gratitude is immeasurable for our patient wives.

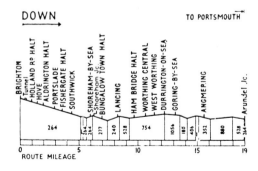

Published to commemorate the golden jubilee of electric traction between London, Brighton and Worthing and also in memory of Henfrey Smail, the local transport historian, from whose researches many have benefitted.

The Ordnance Survey maps reproduced in this album are to the scale of 25 miles to 1 inch.

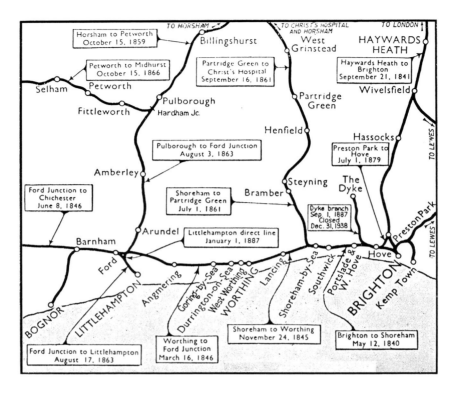

The map contains the following labels:

TO HORSHAM · TO CHRIST'S HOSPITAL AND HORSHAM · TO LONDON

Horsham to Petworth
October 15, 1859

Billingshurst

West Grinstead

HAYWARDS HEATH

Petworth to Midhurst
October 15, 1866

Partridge Green to
Christ's Hospital
September 16, 1861

Haywards Heath to
Brighton
September 21, 1841

Selham

Petworth

Wivelsfield

Pulborough
Hardham Jc.

Partridge Green

Fittleworth

Henfield

Hassocks

Pulborough to Ford Junction
August 3, 1863

Preston Park to
Hove
July 1, 1879

Amberley

Shoreham to
Partridge Green
July 1, 1861

Bramber

Steyning

The Dyke

Dyke branch
Sep. 1, 1887
Closed
Dec. 31, 1938

Ford Junction to
Chichester
June 8, 1846

Arundel

Littlehampton direct line
January 1, 1887

TO LEWES

Preston Park

TO LEWES

Barnham

Ford

BOGNOR · LITTLEHAMPTON · Angmering · Goring-by-Sea · Durrington-on-Sea · West Worthing · WORTHING · Lancing · Shoreham-by-Sea · Southwick · Portslade & W. Hove · Hove · BRIGHTON · Kemp Town

Shoreham to Worthing
November 24, 1845

Brighton to Shoreham
May 12, 1840

Ford Junction to Littlehampton
August 17, 1863

Worthing to
Ford Junction
March 16, 1846

HISTORICAL BACKGROUND

After numerous rival schemes were considered by Parliament an Act was passed on 15th July 1837 authorising the construction of a railway between London and Brighton with branches to Newhaven and Shoreham. The first passenger carrying line in Sussex was the section between Brighton and Shoreham and was opened to the public on 12th May 1840. Opening this length first facilitated the construction of the southern part of the line to London, as materials could be brought in by sea via Shoreham Harbour. Intermediate stations were provided at the following places (approximate population in brackets) Hove (900), Portslade (700), Southwick (500), Kingston (200) and Shoreham (2,000).

It was to be over five years before the route was extended westwards. Trains commenced running to Worthing on November 24th 1845, but with little public celebration.

An alternative route to London came into use in 1861 when a single track from Shoreham to Horsham was opened. A few years later it was doubled and was eventually closed to passengers in 1966.

In April 1874 the "Improved Railway Communication Association" was formed by the disgruntled travellers of Worthing who were tired of the delay caused by all London trains having to reverse at Brighton station. Their pleas for the construction of a bypass curve were ignored and so, undeterred, these stout Victorians presented their own Bill to Parliament. The LBSCR then relented and agreed to build the

Cliftonville spur despite the necessity to tunnel for over 500 yards. It was opened on July 1st 1879.

The publication of this book occurs in the year of the 50th anniversary of the electrification of the London-Brighton-West Worthing route on 1st January 1933. This was a particularly notable historic event as it was generally regarded as the first mainline electrification.

ACCIDENTS

On Sunday, May 17th, 1840, just a week after the opening of the line, a man named Atherall, while riding on the tailboard of a luggage truck which had been pressed into service for the conveyance of passengers, was thrown off and killed between Shoreham and Southwick. This was the first fatal accident on the London & Brighton Railway, and has been often wrongly reported as having happened on the opening day.

In December, 1842, the boiler of an engine named 'Brighton' blew up shortly after passing Hove Station with a train from Brighton to Shoreham. The connecting rods and other parts were blown a considerable distance by the force of the explosion, and were later picked up by the policeman from Hove Station, who arrived on the scene with other helpers attracted to the scene by the report of the explosion. The driver, named William Cavan, was severely scalded about the legs and body, but the fireman escaped injury, and so also did one of the railway engineers, named Meredith, who was travelling on the tender at the time.

An incident occurred in 1844, which reveals the laxity that was then all too prevalent in railway working. At this period there was a regular steamship service between Shoreham, Brighton, and Dieppe, which was run in conjunction with the London & Brighton Railway. When the ship was prevented by the weather from approaching Brighton Pier the railway ran a special train from Shoreham to convey passengers to Brighton. On the evening in question, a special train left Kingston Station at 9 p.m. with passengers for Brighton, and at the same time the usual passenger train left Brighton for Shoreham. By some mismanagement, both trains were sent off on the same line and met head-on between Hove and Southwick. Fortunately the drivers saw each other in time and shut off steam, and at the same time signalled to their guards to apply their brakes, so that a collision was just averted. Both engines were carrying red lamps in front, which seem to have given adequate warning of their approach.

A derailment near Lancing on the opening day of the line to Worthing in 1845 was caused by a train hitting a horse drawn cart.

Since that time there have been no accidents of note on this 10½ mile line—a remarkable record for the generations of railwaymen concerned.

PASSENGER SERVICES

When the service operated only to Shoreham, six return journeys on weekdays were made, with five on Sundays.

By 1869, there were six trains to Portsmouth from Brighton; two to Littlehampton only; six to Horsham and three terminated at Worthing.

In 1890 there were eight Portsmouth and eight Horsham trains, with two running as far as Bognor. There was a 1 hour 35 minute service to London from Worthing in the business hours via the Cliftonville spur.

The 1910 timetable showed seven trains direct between London and the coast line. The 6.10 p.m. from London Bridge slipped the Worthing coaches whilst passing through Haywards Heath but on Saturdays it was the 1.20 p.m. that had slip coaches and they were shed at Horley. There were nine Portsmouth and ten Horsham departures from Brighton together with eleven "Motor Cars" to Worthing, five of which were extended to West Worthing.

1922 saw the commencement of through services to the west with the provision of a Cardiff train, with LSWR and GWR coaches on alternate days. By 1930 through trains to Bournemouth and Plymouth had been introduced.

The advent of electrification in 1933 brought about regular interval services. When this form of traction was extended to Portsmouth in 1938 the hourly direct London trains were extended to Littlehampton and the Brighton departures per hour were three to West Worthing; two to Portsmouth and one to Bognor via Littlehampton.

During World War II there were six trains direct from London to Worthing and an hourly service between Brighton and Portsmouth and between Brighton and Bognor via Littlehampton.

By way of example the morning departures from Brighton in the summer of 1948 are listed below.

9. 3	West Worthing
9.17	Portsmouth slow
9.20	West Worthing
9.27	West Worthing
9.30	Horsham
9.40	Bournemouth West
9.47	Portsmouth fast
9.50	Littlehampton slow
10. 3	West Worthing
10.17	Portsmouth slow
10.20	West Worthing
10.33	West Worthing
10.46	Portsmouth fast
10.49	Littlehampton slow
11. 0	Cardiff
11. 3	West Worthing (Saturdays)
11.17	Portsmouth slow
11.20	West Worthing
11.30	Plymouth

There was an additional hourly service between Littlehampton and London which usually included a Pullman car.

The Bournemouth service was withdrawn during the 1961-2 winter and permanently from September 1963, when the Cardiff train was also taken off. The Plymouth service lasted until 1967 after which it was cut back to Exeter. From October 1971 this remaining service to the West ceased but owing to public pressure was reinstated for the following summer and has run (Saturdays only) ever since. Initially DEMU's from Hastings were used which gave an unadvertised through service from that town but involved reversals at Brighton, Preston Park, Hove and Brighton again. This was due to the fact that whilst platform 3 at Brighton can take trains from the east or west they cannot exceed four coaches. This was sufficient for an experimental daily through service between Portsmouth and Newhaven Harbours in the summer of 1966. That summer there was another unusual through train at 9.12 on Saturdays to Brockenhurst.

One train a week to the West was thought sufficient until 1980 when an additional train on Saturdays to Bristol was introduced. Enterprise was again apparent when this was extended to Cardiff the following year and a 16.20 departure for Bristol on Sundays was introduced. In 1982 the Exeter train was extended to Paignton for the summer months.

The Coastway electric service has been gradually reduced in frequency, notably in 1972. Various changes have been rung—Portsmouth slow trains ran via Littlehampton for a time—West Worthing almost eliminated for termination—pattern of stops varied—all to make for economy of operation. The most recent example is the running of an evening shuttle service between Brighton and Hove only, to connect into the Littlehampton trains from London.

LOCOMOTIVES

The first locomotive was a 2-2-2 named 'Brighton' and was horse drawn from London by road. The second was an 0-4-2 named 'Shoreham', both having been built by Jones, Turner & Evans. The first passenger train was hauled by 'Kingston', a 2-2-2 by Sharp, Roberts & Co.

During the first 30 years of operation trains were hauled by a variety of 2-2-2, 2-4-0, and eventually 0-6-0 locomotives. Brighton Locomotive Works produced its first engine in 1852 and the following year one of them blew up when about to start a train for Littlehampton. By 1870 the LBSCR is believed to have had 72 different classes of locomotive, which were drastically reduced by William Stroudley whose well known designs were to feature strongly on the west coast line for the next 50 years.

Passenger trains were commonly operated by classes B1 (Gladstone), D, E, H and I tanks with A and D tanks on Littlehampton and Horsham trains respectively.

After the railway grouping in 1923 ex-LSWR T9's were often used on the coast line. With the advent of electrification to Portsmouth in 1938 only the West of England and Horsham trains were steam hauled. After World War II the former were often powered by West Country or BR class 4 locomotives and eventually class 33 or 47 diesels. The latter service employed ex-LSWR M7 tanks and then BR class 2 2-6-2's until they were ousted by 3-car DEMU's in the last year of the line.

ELECTRIC STOCK

From the start of electric services from West Worthing, the London service was provided with 6 PUL and 6 PAN units. These 6 coach sets had a pantry car (buffet) or a chocolate and cream-painted Pullman car in their formation, photographs of which we plan to include in the next album in this series. Local services were provided by elderly ex-LSWR 3 coach sets initially, later replaced by 2 BIL and 2 HAL units, which lasted until 1971. They were displaced by 4 COR sets for a year or so until the arrival of the present 2 HAP s and 4 VEP s. The PUL s and PAN s retired in 1965-6 to make way for the current 4 CIG and 4 BIG units.

THE FUTURE

In 1976 the Transport 2000 Southern Group published an integrated transport strategy for the South Coast. It envisaged the down line being used by light rail vehicles of one or two car units of the type more recently introduced on the Tyne and Wear Metro and the up line being used for the longer distance BR trains, with additional passing loops on both lines. The plan shows stage I of the scheme which was again aired at the motorway enquiry in 1982.

The coal concentration depot that was opened at Hove in 1970 is to be improved, financed by a £180,000 Department of Transport grant announced in September 1982.

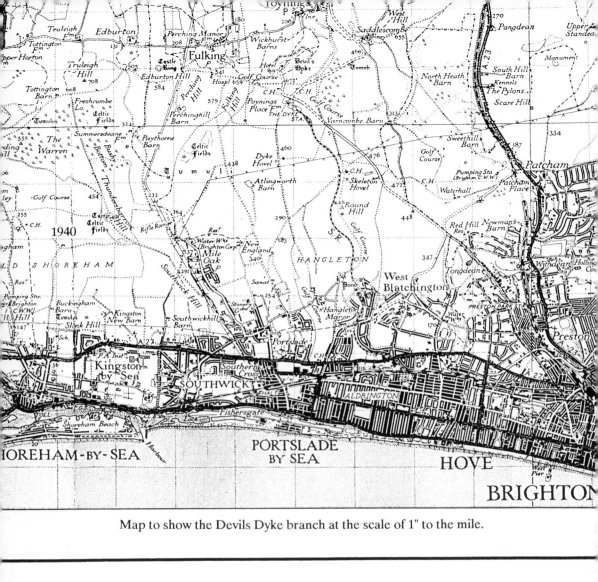

Map to show the Devils Dyke branch at the scale of 1" to the mile.

1″ to the mile scale maps showing the urbanisation of the Brighton to Shoreham area. Hove grew rapidly after the opening of the Cliftonville spur in 1879, no doubt due to some degree to the improved communications with London.

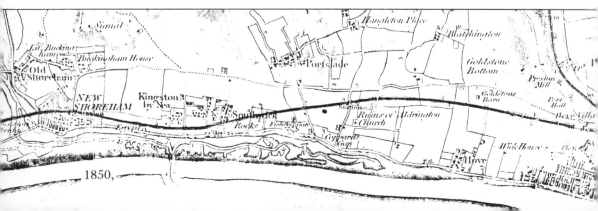

1872,

1882,

1898,

1912.

BRIGHTON

An artist's impression of the exterior of the station soon after its completion. The building is little changed today although partly obscured by the forecourt roof. Construction was not started until some months after the opening of the Shoreham line in May 1840.

(C. Fry collection)

April 1842
timetable
and fares.

FARES.					
1st Class.		2d Class.		3d Class.	
s.	d.	s.	d.	s.	d.
1	0	0	9	0	6
1	0	0	9	0	6

	DAILY, except Sundays.						Sunday Trains.			
	A.M. h. m. 	A.M. h. m.	NOON. h. m.	P.M. h. m.	P.M. h. m.	P.M. h. m.	A.M. h. m.	P.M. h. m.	P.M. h. m.	P.M. h. m.
From BRIGHTON.	7.30	9.30	12.15	2.45	4.45	7. 0	9. 0	2.15	3.45	5.15
From SHOREHAM.	8.30	10.30	1. 0	3.30	5.30	7.30	10. 0	2.45	4.30	6. 0

A well known print by H. G. Hine which was described as "in commemoration of the opening of the Shoreham Branch". One account of the opening, however, states that "there were no station buildings nor even platforms". Another report was as follows:–

It was Monday, May 11, 1840, and at three o'clock in the afternoon the very first Sussex train pulled out of Brighton Station on its way to Shoreham. On this opening day, admission was by ticket only and a select company of 230 people were privileged to make the first trip.

The band of the 12th Lancers played and the first train passengers, amidst smoke and steam, disappeared into the distance. The train consisted of an engine known as the "Kingston" to which were coupled six carriages and three luggage wagons.

The men passengers in their tall hats and peg-top trousers and the ladies in their flounced skirts and parasols sat and stood in these primitive wagons. They would have a more or less uninterrupted view of the Channel on their left as the engine puffed along on its five and a half mile journey with speed building up to 20 m.p.h.

There was little difference in the standards of comfort among the three classes of passenger. All were subjected to the soot, smoke, sparks and steam of these early locomotives. The first class passengers were a little better protected in that they were roofed in, but had no windows. The second class trucks were open, but had seating. But most of the third class trucks had no seats at all.

The first train journey from Brighton to Shoreham took 12 minutes and the return journey 15 minutes. There was a Grande Fete to celebrate the opening of this new railway — held that night at the "Swiss Gardens." The "Swiss Gardens," now just a memory, had been opened two years before. With their palatial gardens and ballroom larger than anything else on the South Coast it was the right place for such an important celebration. Shoreham was indeed honoured.

After the official opening of this new Sussex Railway, the fare-paying passengers could look forward to a two-hourly service. The train from Brighton to Shoreham ran every two hours from 9 o'clock to 7 o'clock and from Shoreham 10 o'clock to 8 o'clock. On the first official public open day 1,750 passengers were carried.

1. The erection of the splendid curved train shed that we can admire today was undertaken in 1882/3 and this photograph shows work in progress before the earlier roofs were removed. It also reveals much detail of contemporary coaches and signalling together with one line that has two platforms.
(National Railway Museum)

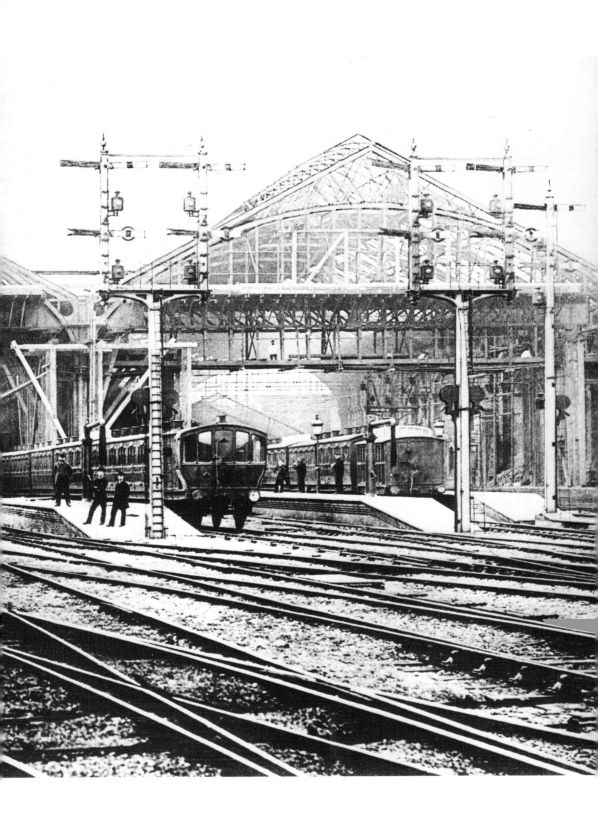

2.   An eastward view from above the tunnel mouth of the Worthing line in 1859 showing the locomotive works and running shed adjacent to the London line. The chalk hill
was gradually removed to make way for new carriage and loco running sheds, erection
starting in 1861.   (C. Fry collection)

3.   A view from the same location about 75 years later after the introduction of electric
traction in 1933 showing not only the expansion of railway premises but also of Brighton.
Note the electric tram on the New England Road bridge and the then new colour light
signal in the cutting.   (C. Fry collection)

4.   Whilst great attention was paid to ornamental detail in the roof and stanchion design it seems that little thought was given to the confusion that would result from giving two platform faces the same number. The matter had been reconsidered by the time the photograph no. 10 was taken. Notice the 4-wheel carriages and the "Registration Office for Continental Baggage, Excess Baggage, Horses, Carriages and Dogs".

(National Railway Museum)

NEW ENGLAND TUNNEL.

5. Photo taken in 1903–The premises had been acquired by the LBSCR in 1877. They were sold to the Corporation for street widening in 1923 and subsequently demolished. The bus stand is now sited here.   (National Railway Museum)

7. A superb display of vintage transport and lighting equipment outside Brighton station. The clock and upper windows of the 1841 building can be seen in front of the train shed roof. The lowest roof, the porte cochère, was added around 1882.

(Lens of Sutton)

6.   A snap of Terminus Road with a row of waiting cabs and the corner of the station
in the late 19th century.   (M. J. Joly collection)

8.   The locomotive running shed in LBSCR days with two steam cranes for coaling the engines. It was located between the London and West Coast lines. The East Coast line can be seen curving away in the distance on the right.   (C. Fry collection)

9.   Overlooking the west coast line we see the side of the loco shed and part of the coal store. The small building without a roof beyond the turntable is the well ventilated locomen's toilet block.   (B. C. Vigor collection)

10.   The unveiling of the War Memorial to the railway staff lost in World War I. At this time the refreshment rooms were operated under licence by Bertram & Co. On the right is the ticket barrier at which our journey westwards will commence.
                                                                    (M. J. Joly collection)

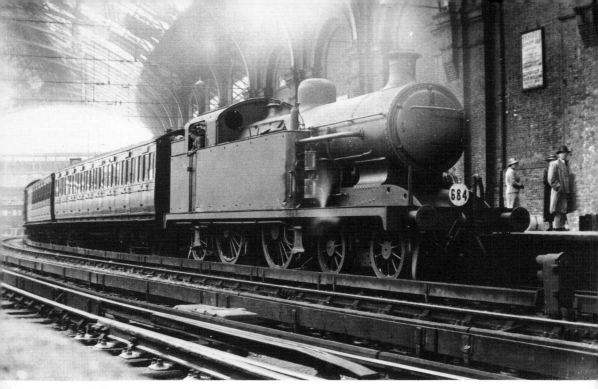

11.   Most westbound trains leave from platforms 1 or 2, but the points in the foreground permit short trains to leave from no. 3. Here we see a rebuilt I1 4-4-2 tank about to leave no. 2 in primer having just come out of the works for a test run.

(C. Fry collection)

13.   The view from Brighton South signalbox looking towards Hove in 1924, with the
New England cabin to the right of the road bridge of the same name.   (Late E. Wallis)

12.   On the left is class I3 no. B91 and on the right class I1x no. B603. They are posed
in 1929 outside the loco shed and make an interesting comparison in methods of
securing smokebox doors.   (Lens of Sutton)

14.   A birds-eye view from the top of the train shed roof showing the end of platforms 1 and 2, the running sheds, west signal box in the foreground and south signalbox immediately to the right. The Portsmouth lines are on the left and the London lines on the right of this picture taken in 1924, nine years before the signal boxes were closed down.   (Late E. Wallis)

16.   Class K no. 32350 about to leave platform 2 with a through train to the West on 23rd June, 1956. The first coach is in "plum and custard" livery which contrasted sharply with the prevalent all green electric stock.   (H. C. Casserley)

15.   The locomotive running shed in BR days. Not strictly true as this picture was taken during the long railway strike in the summer of 1955. The slate roof and arches had been replaced in 1938.   (E. Gamblin)

17.   West Country class "Launceston" no. 34012 at the head of a special train to Blandford Forum on 11th June 1966–thought to have been the last steam passenger train from Brighton. Some of the connections to the loco shed had already been removed by then, for although it had officially been closed in 1964, it was still occasionally used until demolished in 1966.   (J. Scrace)

18.   Waiting to leave platform 2 is a 4 CEP unit normally used on Kent coast services. This is an unusual emu for the Central Division's Coastway service to Bognor in 1969. The very short plat-form near the wall was used to load supplies of cutlery, crockery, linen, etc., into Pullman cars after their overhaul in the nearby works.   (J. A. M. Vaughan)

HOLLAND ROAD HALT

This was one of a number of halts opened on 3rd September 1905 to be served by the "Motor Trains" to Worthing. The LBSCR took every opportunity to counteract the adverse effect the new electric tramways were having on their traffic receipts. The halt was closed on 7th May 1956 and was the only one on the coast line to retain its timber decking.

19. The ubiquitous Terrier locomotive was introduced to operate the company's London suburban services and was soon to be found all over their system. The wooden steps up to Holland Road can be seen above the locomotive's coal bunker. (M. J. Joly collection)

The first Hove station was situated at Holland Road from 1840 to 1880 and is shown on this 1873 six inch scale map.

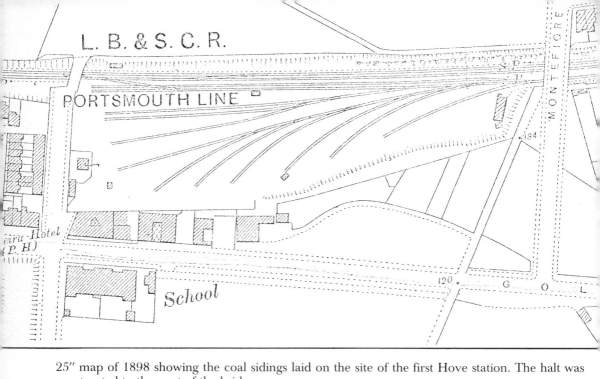

L. B. & S. C. R.

PORTSMOUTH LINE

25″ map of 1898 showing the coal sidings laid on the site of the first Hove station. The halt was constructed to the west of the bridge

20. Viewed from Holland Road bridge in June 1953 we see class C2X no. 32440 hauling empty stock from Brighton to Hove past the site of the first Hove station. (P. Hay)

21.   Holland Road was served by the ½-hourly electric service, all stations and halts, to West Worthing, seen here on Saturday 17th March 1956.   (E. Wilmshurst)

22.   The halt was also served by one or two Horsham trains in the rush hour. M7 no. 30053 is about to stop with the 1.50 p.m. from Brighton on the same day. In the age of the 5½ day week, Saturday lunchtime was regarded as a rush hour.   (E. Wilmshurst)

HOVE

The first station was situated to the east of Holland Road and was opened with the line on 12th May 1840, closing on 1st March 1880. A station at the present site was opened on 1st October 1865 and was named Cliftonville and West Brighton, being changed to Hove and West Brighton in 1893. In the same year a new booking hall was built to the west of the original premises and two years later the name became plain Hove.

THREE-ARCH BRIDGE, CONNECTING MR. STANFORD'S
PROPERTY AT HOVE.

Plan and elevation, dated April 1840, produced at the dawn of the railway age and containing a number of curious features. The office had only a counter, without the partition and small window found necessary in later booking offices for reasons of security. The gentlemen's WC's are separated from the urinal by the ladies' rooms. Hardly a convenient convenience. The provision of a cesspool immediately under the windows must have been another rather unattractive feature in an otherwise elegant little building. (C. Fry collection)

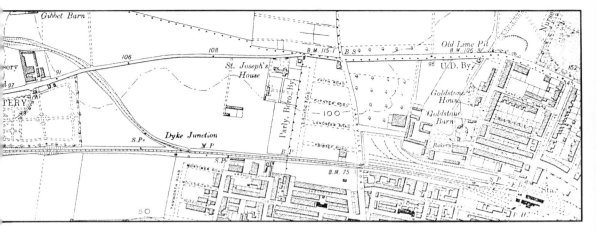

Six inch scale map of 1899. The goods yard was later extended further north.

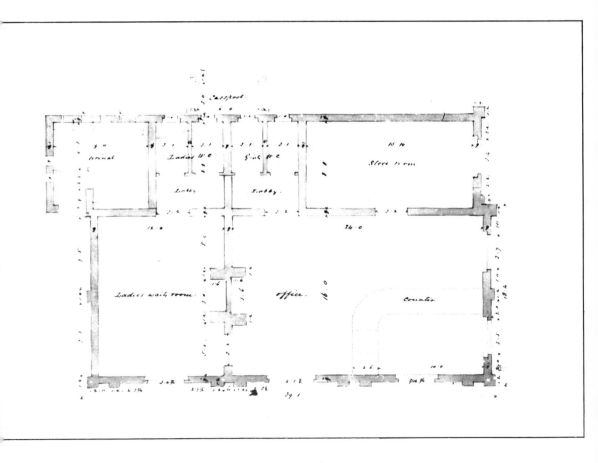

23.   Hove at its zenith with the 1865 building on the right and the 1893 structure, both
with canopies. The covered footbridge rises between the two buildings and was primarily
a public footpath, a subway being provided for passengers.   (Lens of Sutton)

24.   The 1893 station building was mainly a spacious booking hall and is seen here
before erection of the ornate porte-cochère to give shelter to passengers transferring to
road transport.   (Lens of Sutton)

25.   The original company's initials survive to this day in glazed tiles in the support of the porte-cochère. The steel structure was second-hand when it was erected at Hove, having served a similar purpose outside Victoria station before the reconstruction of that station.   (E. Wilmshurst)

26. The elegant round-headed windows and doorways of the 1865 station look at their best after redecoration in 1970.   (J. Minnis)

THE PULLMAN CAR COMPANY LTD

The holder M_____

is entitled to travel in a
FIRST CLASS PULLMAN CAR
between the undermentioned stations

VICTORIA, LONDON BRIDGE,
Nº   CHARING CROSS   Amount
                                                    Paid
513   AND
            HOVE   £

for the period
_____ 19___ to _____ 19_____

ISSUED SUBJECT TO THE CONDITIONS
SET OUT ON THE BACK HEREOF

28. The approach to the up side has changed little since this postcard was produced in 1911, although the small booking office at the end of the shops is no longer used.
(Lens of Sutton)

27. This fine class D1 (no. 268) is a splendid example of the pride taken at Brighton Locomotive Works in finishing the paintwork of their creations. The practice of naming locomotives after villages in the area of the LBSCR sometimes caused confusion with passengers who thought the train was going to the place named. Baynards was described in our previous album "Branch lines to Horsham".   (Lens of Sutton)

29.   One of the successful class D1 0-4-2 tank locomotives no. 362 passing under the foot-bridge which crosses all the running lines, platforms and sidings. The guard's van in the platform is displaying the LV board which indicated that it was the last vehicle in the train. More recently a white painted lamp with red glass has indicated to railway staff that the train is complete and has not shed any vehicles en route.   (C. Fry collection)

30.   Class I1 no. 9 entering Hove circa. 1908 from the west past the goods yard which contains wagons of two local coal merchants – Price & Co. and Wm. Colwell.
                                        (M. P. Bennett collection/Bluebell Archives)

31.   Gladstone class no. 215 on the only quadruple track on the Sussex coast, again circa. 1908. The train has just come off the Cliftonville spur and is about to enter Hove station.

(M. P. Bennett collection/Bluebell Archives)

32.   Class I3 89 (later numbered 2089) entering the up island platform in the mid-1930's. A large part of the lengthy footbridge is visible.   (Lens of Sutton)

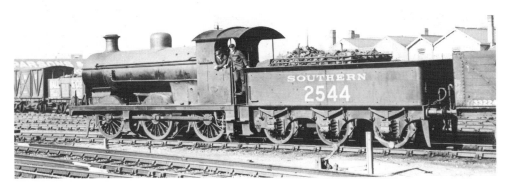

33.   The afternoon sun in October 1934 illuminates class C2X no. 2544 to good advant-
age at the entrance to the goods yard.   (H. C. Casserley)

34.   The through train from Bournemouth is seen here in August 1955 passing Hove
'A' Box. The leading coach is an ex-LSWR first/third of 1924 with the unusual outside
frame bogies, examples of which survive today on the Mid-Hants Railway. Hove signals
are even today still a mixture of semaphore and colour light. The locomotive is class H2
no. 32424.   (P. Hay)

35.   Despite what Northerners think the South Coast does have heavy snow from time
to time. Brighton shed kept this C class no. 31724 ready for work in March 1956.
(E. Gamblin)

36.   With snow already up to rail level a Portsmouth bound electric is seen here entering Hove on the penultimate day of 1962 during what was to become the worst winter
in living memory, when even the sea froze.   (E. Wilmshurst)

37.   In store in Hove goods yard during January 1963 was E6 no. 32418, E4 no. 32479, E6 no. 32417, K no. 32342, K no. 32341, Schools class no. 30923 "Bradfield". Coal froze in wagons and much of British industry was at a standstill for over two months.   (E. Wilmshurst)

38.   Hove 'B' stood at the west end of the station acting as a block post and controlling access to the goods yard and nearby sidings.   (J. Scrace)

DYKE JUNCTION (Aldrington Halt from 17th June 1932)

Opened on 3rd September 1905

39.   Terrier no. 79 "Minories" with the Worthing to Brighton motor train at the junction with the Dyke branch which can be seen on the right. Note the vast difference in the profiles of locomotive and coach.   (M. P. Bennett collection/Bluebell Archives)

Map of 1911.

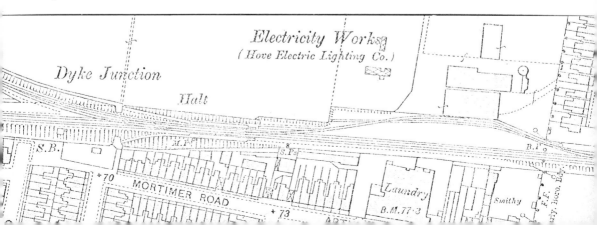

40.   Class C3 no. 303 on a trial trip stops near Dyke Junction Halt in 1906 for smoke-box door inspection amidst the wide open undeveloped fields.

(M. P. Bennett collection/Bluebell Archives)

41. Terrier no. 79 propels its coach towards the junction signalbox over the trailing crossover normally used by freight trains leaving the electricity works sidings.

(C. Fry collection)

42. Railmotor no. 2 leaves the halt on its way to Brighton. Amongst the passengers' complaints about this unit were vibration from the engine; dirt, because it was kept in the loco shed and not the carriage shed and overcrowding, because it was not powerful enough to haul another coach at busy times. (C. Fry collection)

43. Sentinel railcar no. 6 did not produce so much vibration and lasted longer than no. 2 on the Dyke branch. It had wooden wheel centres to reduce noise but this created problems with track circuit operation and necessitated the provision of lorry-type brake drums. It is seen here in October 1933, five months after its introduction. (H. C. Casserley)

44. A Brighton to Littlehampton service arrives in 1982 at the concrete platform which had replaced the original timber one. The unit is one of the 4 VEP type first introduced in 1967.
(J. Scrace)

THE DYKE BRANCH

This 3 mile long branch to the summit of the South Downs at the Devils Dyke was on an almost continuous gradient of 1 in 40 and was opened on 1st September 1887. The area was very thinly populated and the line was intended for the use of visitors to this well known beauty spot.

The first halt on the branch was opened in 1891 only 62 chains from the terminus and was for the use of the Golf Club. An electric bell in the clubhouse rang automatically when the starting signal at the station was lowered to advise intending passengers to drink up.

The other halt on the branch was brought into use on 12th January 1934 to serve housing developments. Being situated behind Rowan Avenue, it was named Rowan Halt and was the terminating point for about half the motor trains in the final winters of the line. Closure was on the last day of 1938.

A detailed history is given by Paul Clark in "The Railways of the Devils Dyke" (Turntable Publications 1976).

45. The scene after the arrival of class E3 no. 168 at the small corrugated iron terminal buildings before running round its train. Owing to the severe gradient regulations demanded that the locomotive be on the descending end of the train.   (Lens of Sutton)

46.   A view of the terminus showing its exposed and isolated location. The small goods yard received some coal and cattle food and sent out little more than an occasional load of hay. A disused coach body served as a summer tea room.   (C. Fry collection)

47.   D class no. 228 "Seaford" about to run round its train, the headboards and tailboards having already been positioned for the return journey. The high elliptical roof line of the bogie coaches earned them the nickname "Balloons".   (C. Fry collection)

48.   E4 class no. 2505 leaving the station intent on wearing its brake blocks a little thinner. The background completes the picture of the relative isolation of this terminus.

(C. Fry collection)

SOUTHERN RAILWAY.
ONE DOG AT OWNER'S RISK (accompanied by Passenger)
BETWEEN
BRIGHTON and THE DYKE
RATE 3d.
This Ticket is available for one journey only and must be given up at destination Station
The Passenger is requested to see this ticket punched at the time of issue.
FOR CONDITIONS SEE BACK.

1905.

		Week Days.												Sundays.						

BRIGHTON and THE DYKE (Motor Cars—One class only).—L. B. and S. C.

Miles.		Week Days.					Except Sats.	aft	Sats.	aft	aft	aft	mrn	mrn	aft	aft	aft	aft		
		n	mrn	mrn	aft	aft		aft								Sundays.				
	Central Station, Brighton ¶ ....dep.	10 0	11 3	1158	1250	1 45		2 35		2 40	4 40	5 50	10 0	1152	40 3	35	4 30	6 25		
1¼	Hove ¶	10 9	11 9	12 4	1256	1 51		2 41		2 46	4 46	5 56	10 6	1121	2 46	3 41	4 36	6 31		
5½	The Dyke .... arr.	1025	1123	1218	1 10	2 5		2 55		3 0	5 0	6 10	1020	1135	3 0	3 55	4 50	6 45		

Miles.		Week Days.										Sundays.						
		n	mrn	aft	aft	aft	aft	aft				mrn	aft	aft	aft	aft	aft	
	The Dyke ¶ ....dep.	1045	1128	1225	1 20	2 10	4 15	5 10	6 15			1030	5 3	5 4	0 5	15	7 0	
4	Hove ¶	11 1	1141	1238	1 33	2 23	4 28	5 23	6 28			1043	18 3	18 4	13 5	23 7	13	
5½	Brighton (C.).. arr.	11 6	1147	1244	1 39	2 29	4 34	5 29	6 34			1049	24 3	24 4	19 5	31 7	19	

n 1, 2, and 3 class Trains; not stopping at the Halts.
¶ "Halts" at Holland Road, between Brighton and Hove; and Dyke Junction, between Hove and The Dyke.

49. The station staff normally consisted of one man who acted as booking clerk, porter, signalman and shunter. There was an electric train staff for the safe working of the single line. This photograph taken in August 1924 shows the Saxby and Farmer 15-lever rocker frame box. (Late E. Wallis)

50. The evening sun gave the photographer a good opportunity to record the running gear of class I2 no. 14. These engines were a little "light-footed" for the 1 in 40 gradient, locomen preferring the six coupled machines, particularly the E4's. (C. Fry collection)

PORTSLADE AND WEST HOVE

51.   An official view of the present station when new in 1882. The original down platform was on the opposite side of the level crossing. The signal is of the slotted post type
and its lamp with coloured glasses was rotated by cranks and illuminated by gas.

(C. Fry collection)

6″ scale map showing the sidings and rural location of Portslade station in 1899.

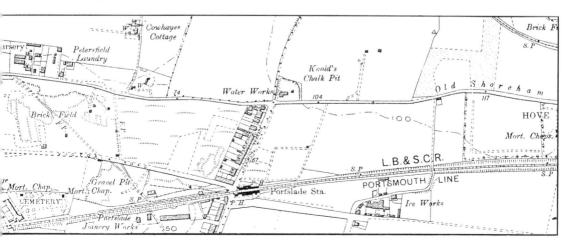

52.   Terrier no. 81 "Beaulah" passes under Olive Road bridge circa. 1906. It is running as an 2-4-0 instead of an 0-6-0 tank.   (M. P. Bennett collection/Bluebell Archives)

53.   The ladies on the bus are gazing at the elegant southern façade of the station. The small canopy over the approach steps survived until 1981. Behind the houses Green's set up their sponge cake-mix factory which had its own railway siding.   (Lens of Sutton)

54. Some years after the LBSCR moved its carriage works from Brighton to Lancing it was forced by strike action to provide a special train each day for the workmen, which became known unofficially as the "Lancing Belle". It is seen here on the 5th June 1962, hauled by E4 tanks nos. 32503 and 32468, obscuring the goods shed and yard, which included a siding for Ronuk's polish factory. Goods traffic ceased in 1968.

(E. Wilmshurst)

55.   Portslade signalbox is adjacent to the level crossing and is a block post with mainly sema-phore signals. The down advance home however has been changed to electric and moved to the end of the platform at Fishersgate Halt. This small cabin used to be on the down side of the goods yard.   (C. Fry collection)

57. A 2HAP unit leads a semi-fast train from Portsmouth into the up platform. The up side buildings have been leased out, so that passengers now have to wait in an open shelter. This view was taken from the footbridge in March 1982. (J. Scrace)

56. A 2BIL set passes over the level crossing on its way to Littlehampton on 28th April 1969. The starting signal has now lost its upper arm as "signal visibility" has been improved with the removal of the station awning. (J. Scrace)

FISHERSGATE HALT

One of the 1905 series of Rail Motor Halts designed to serve the expanding urban areas.

58.   The Balloon coach of a Motor Train almost obscures the locomotive hauling it. Even today trains that can be worked in either direction show a head code and tail lamp at the same time, as is seen here.   (Lens of Sutton)

59.   Today it is one of the few remaining halts that is still staffed.   (J. Scrace)

SOUTHWICK

London Brighton & South Coast Railway.

Southwick to

Balcombe

60.   The original building was replaced by the one illustrated in the 1890's. This in turn was superseded by the present structure in 1971. We have no explanation for the cannon that appears to be a threat to errant signalmen. Note the splendid topiary on the embankment.   (Lens of Sutton)

61.   Looking towards the sea at the Shoreham end of the station it is interesting to reflect that carts loaded with baskets of shellfish stood where the pram is now seen. A hand operated crane hoisted the merchandise up to the platform. Headroom now 12′ 4″.

(National Railway Museum)

63.   Loco. no. E6047 hauls a Chichester to Selhurst special train consisting of electric units nos. 3135, 3142 and 3111 on 28th April 1973. This was probably the first stage of their journey from the South Coast to the scrapyard. Notice the covered slopes from the subway to the platforms.   (J. Scrace)

52.   Class C2X no. 32534 about to pass over the subway with a Horsham train consisting of a SECR and LBSCR coach with a van at the rear.   (P. Hay)

KINGSTON WHARF

A station was provided at Kingston when the railway was opened and was used by ferry passengers to and from France when the weather was unsuitable for the ship to call at Brighton pier. When the LBSCR acquired this shipping route it transferred it to Newhaven. Kingston station was closed in 1879.

The wharf sidings were linked to the coast line by an incline operated by a steam winding engine on the north side of the track and a number of wagon turntables were provided.

This map of 1893 shows the railway coke ovens which originally produced coke for the locomotives. They were demolished at this time and two extra sidings laid in their place. Note the street tramway.

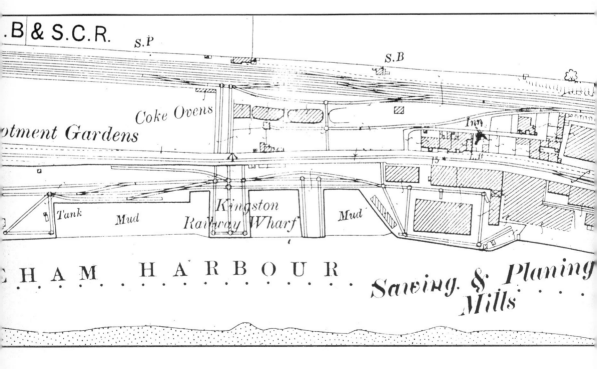

THE VIADUCT AT KINGSTON.

64.   LBSCR coal wagons stand on the 2-road jetty shown on the map, whilst the harbour entrance can be seen in this photograph (circa. 1908) beyond the masts of the sailing vessel.   (J. R. Minnis collection)

65.   At the same time a steamship is moored at the end of the 3-road jetty in the company of a steam crane.

(J. R. Minnis collection)

→

67.   The incline, looking up towards the chimney of the winding house, with a turntable in the
foreground. Work had just commenced on the construction of an oblique line on a 1 in 82
gradient to replace the incline when this photograph was taken by the site engineer in 1938.
The white area remained on the arch after a small building had been demolished.   (D. J. Taylor)

66.   Horses were used until 1938 for shunting the wharf and top sidings. The shunter is not hold-
ing a weapon for use on the poor animal but a sprague for chocking or moving wagon wheels.
(Lens of Sutton)

68. The reconstruction involved filling in the spaces between the jetties with shingle from Dungeness and piling a straight frontage to the wharf. Clearly seen is the gentle slope of the main road bridge (A259) and the encroaching shingle in the basin. (H. M. Madgwick)

69. The first steam train onto the wharf. Goodbye to the horses at last. The new water frontage is in line with the buffers of the ex-SECR P class tank. (D. J. Taylor)

70. Class D3 no. 32390 speeds past the Kingston Wharf box towards Horsham in April 1953.   (P. Hay)

		BRIGHTON and WEST WORTHING—(Motor Cars—One class only).— L. B. & S. C.																				
Miles	Up. Central Station.		Week Days.													Sundays.						
			mrn	mrn	mrn	aft	aft	aft	aft	aft	aft	aft	aft			aft	mrn	mrn	mrn	aft	aft	aft	aft	aft	aft
	Brighton ¶ ¶ ......dep.	6 35	9 10	10 30	12 5	12 40	2 20	4 0	5 40	6 50	7 29	8 25		10 0	8 10	9 20	10 50	12 5	1 15	2 45	4 10	5 50	7 20
1½	Hove ¶ ¶	6 41	9 16	10 36	12 9	12 46	2 26	4 6	5 46	6 56	7 26	8 31		10 4	8 16	9 26	10 56	12 9	1 21	2 51	4 16	5 56	7 26
3	Portslade ¶ ¶	6 45	9 20	10 40	....	12 50	2 30	4 10	5 50	7 0	7 30	8 35		10 7	8 20	9 30	11 0	....	1 25	2 55	4 20	6 0	7 30
4½	Southwick	6 49	9 24	10 44	....	12 54	2 34	4 14	5 54	7 4	7 34	8 39		10 10	8 24	9 34	11 4	....	1 29	2 59	4 24	6 4	7 34
6	Shoreham-by-Sea ‡ ...	6 53	9 28	10 48	12 18	12 58	2 38	4 18	5 58	7 8	7 38	8 43		10 14	8 28	9 38	11 8	12 18	1 33	3 3	4 28	6 8	7 38
8½	Lancing ¶ ¶	6 58	9 34	10 54	....	1 4	2 44	4 24	6 4	7 14	7 44	8 49		10 20	8 34	9 44	11 14	....	1 38	3 9	4 34	6 14	7 44
10½	Worthing ¶ ¶	7 4	9 40	11 0	12 26	1 10	2 50	4 30	6 10	7 20	7 50	8 55		10 25	8 40	9 50	11 20	12 26	1 45	3 15	4 40	6 20	7 50
11½	West Worthing § .. arr.	....	9 43	....	....	1 13	2 53	....	....	....	7 53	8 58		....	....	....	....	....	....	....	....	....	....

‡ Station for Lancing College (2 miles); § for West Tarring (½ mile).
¶¶ "Halts" at Holland Road, between Brighton and Hove; Dyke Junction, between Hove and Portslade; Fishersgate, between Portslade and Southwick; Ham Bridge, between Lancing and Worthing.
☞ For OTHER TRAINS and Motor Cars between Brighton and Shoreham-by-Sea, see page 195.
∴ For OTHER TRAINS between Brighton and West Worthing, see pages 176 to 189.

71. Two years later another Horsham train is seen a little to the east of the previous location. The loco is ex-LSWR M7 no. 30031; the coaches are an ex-LSWR composite and an ex-SECR 10-compartment third; the house was formerly that of Kingston station and the ventilators behind it are part of the Kemp Town Brewery malthouses. (P. Hay)

72. 21 years after the first P class tank came onto the wharf the same class was still at work there. 31556, formerly SR no. 556, is seen here on the diamond crossing put in when the turntables were removed. (W. M. J. Jackson)

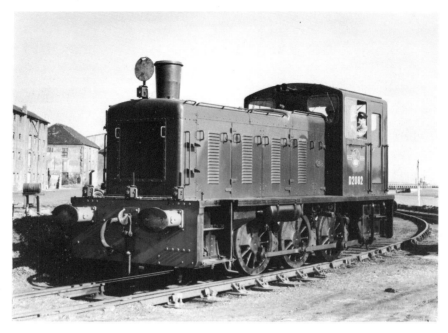

73.   Two months later a diesel shunter, now classified 03, arrived and was well suited to the sharp curves with its mere 9ft. wheelbase. Freight traffic ceased 9 years later in 1968.

(W. M. J. Jackson)

74.   Approaching Kingston Wharf sidings on 7th October 1962 is class K no. 32353 hauling a railway enthusiasts special.   (S. C. Nash)

SHOREHAM

75.   The first station here appears to be identical to that which we have seen at Hove. There is a short flight of steps up to the platform and one notice board displays "Bye-laws" and the other "List of Tolls". This 1870 view shows three early types of signal—a three position home and starter on the right; a revolving disc distant beyond the gates, and to its left, in the distance, are the junction splitting signals.   (National Railway Museum)

Train departure times in 1853.

SHOREHAM.

	UP TRAINS.—DAILY.											SUNDAYS.				
SHOREHAM ...	7 49	8 20	10 25	1 7	3 17	...		5 30	6 25	8 0	10 15	7 59	2 10	5 40	6 25	8 56
Brighton	9 0	8 45	11 0	1 45	4 0	...		6 0	7 0	8 35	10 30	8 20	2 30	6 15	5 45	9 30
London	11 30	10 5	1 0	3 45	5 45	...		—	9 5	10 30	——	10 30	4 20	9 0	—	—

	DOWN TRAINS.															
SHOREHAM ...	7 30	8 50	9 20	11 55	1 35	2 20	...	4 35	5 45	7 35	9 30	9 50	10 50	2 12	3 20	8 35
Chichester.........	—	9 50	—	12 40	—	3 7	...	—	6 42	8 30		10 55	...	3 2	...	9 35
Portsmouth		10 35		1 20		3 35	....		7 15	8 15		13 40	...	3 60	...	10 20

STEYNING.—A COACH leaves Steyning, for Shoreham in time to meet the 8.30 a.m. train from Portsmouth, returning from Shorenam on the arrival of the 5.35 p.m. train from Brighton.

77.   Looking towards Brighton in 1886 with ballast over the sleepers! This practice was eventually prohibited by the Board of Trade as it could conceal defective timbers.

(National Railway Museum)

76. These first improvements to the station included raising the platforms, fencing off the old building, provision of a subway and erection of a new signal box, all of which can be seen in this 1886 view.   (National Railway Museum)

78.   An Edwardian postcard captures the action outside the Burrell Arms as the gates close in front of a car and a horse drawn water cart. Notice that the Steyning branch signal is higher than the coast line one, an arrangement that the SR reversed – see photo 80.   (Wise collection)

79.   Another postcard of that period shows an unexpected occurrence, which is self explanatory. Don't overlook the sizeable vessels beached on the eastern shore.

(West Sussex Reference Library)

80.   For five years after the electrification to West Worthing in 1933, Portsmouth trains continued to be steam hauled. Here I3 class no. 2022 coasts past Shoreham B Box with a train displaying four guard's duckets (look outs), common before the introduction of periscopes on the electric stock. Other views of this location appear in our earlier book "Branch Lines to Horsham".

(Lens of Sutton)

81.   The incongruity of a steam hauled lengthy goods train rumbling past a strangely deserted goods yard and the elderly gas lamps of a modernised electric railway was one of the charms of this railway scene.

(Lens of Sutton)

82.   Class C2X no. 32529 struggling with 9.02 freight from Hove to Beeding Cement Works on 11th April 1959. The train consists of empty cement wagons and loaded coal trucks. The poor engine seems to be discharging a lot of steam from its private parts. Shoreham goods yard closed in 1965.   (W. M. J. Jackson)

83.   Shoreham A Box was situated opposite the goods yard, with the traditional toilet under the steps.   (J. Scrace)

84.   E6036, now classified 73, on an up freight train on 28th April 1972. These versatile locomotives produce 1600 HP from their electric motors and when running off the electrified system
they can retract their collector shoes and generate 600 HP from their diesel engines.   (J. Scrace)

85.   The attractive architecture of the south side of a station that any town could be proud of.
(J. Scrace)

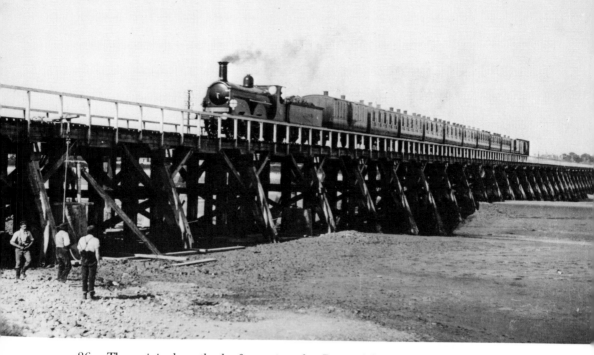

86. The original method of crossing the River Adur was by this elaborate timber viaduct. Two of the workmen are taking an interest in the Gladstone class locomotive and the train of oil lit coaches, whilst the other one turns his back on the passengers to adjust his trousers. (Lens of Sutton)

87. West Country class "Ottery St. Mary" crosses the replacement bridge built in 1911 with a West of England train 27th August 1952. (Lens of Sutton)

Parliament demanded that every railway should have one train per day which would carry passengers at one penny per mile, hence this parliamentary ticket. The obverse was dated 7 AUG 83.

London Brighton & South Coast Railway.

Shoreham-by-Sea to

Emsworth

88. A contemporary scene as a down train rumbles over the bridge and the mist lifts to reveal the ornate buildings of Lancing College with its immense Chapel perched on the cut edge of the South Downs, where that lengthy chalk structure has been severed by the erosive River Adur. (J. A. M. Vaughan)

SHOREHAM AIRPORT

89.   This is believed to be the first airport station in the country but was opened as Bungalc
Town Halt on 1st October 1910 to serve the sprawl of cheap dwellings scattered on the west si
of the river at about this time. A major component of these buildings was shown crossing t
river in photo no. 79. The halt was closed with the advent of electrification and was reopened
the Airport station (as illustrated), on 1st July 1935. The train passing through is the noon depa

...re from Brighton to Plymouth on 11th May 1938. Air services were operated to Jersey, Birming-
...am and Liverpool, the latter two routes being run by Railway Air Services Ltd., on behalf of
...he GWR and SR. The airfield was developed in World War I and became vital in World War II.
...he station was closed for good on 15th June 1940 for reasons of security.   (H. M. Madgwick)

LANCING

The small village nestled on the Upper Brighton Road when the railway arrived and offered it a station ¾ of a mile to the south. South Lancing developed around it and eventually the two merged together. This remote venue was the surprising location for the LBSCR's new carriage works built in 1912 on a massive 66 acre site, between the railway and the coast.

90.   The rural setting of the attractive flint and brick buildings is well portrayed in this undated view of the station level crossing and up starting signal, looking north.

(Lens of Sutton)

91. Looking west at about the same time we see class DI no. 361 blowing off, about to start a train to Brighton, the cyclist having only one finger free to reduce the noise level. Early train spotters seem more interested in the rare site of a camera. (C. Fry collection)

92. A rare view of an LBSCR freight train on the coast line. An eastbound train of empties waits for the crossing gates to be opened. Note the dumb buffers and the flaps protecting the axle boxes. (Lens of Sutton)

93.   A mid-thirties glimpse eastwards from the steps of the footbridge showing the only siding on this side of the station and an ornate telephone kiosk of the period.   (Lens of Sutton)

94.   Permanent way work in progress in the November mist of 1959 whilst a 2BIL set passes on its way from Brighton. On the right is the goods yard whilst the lines on the left lead to the carriage works.   (E. Wilmshurst)

95. When the SR introduced their Schools class passenger locomotives they sought additional publicity by having the naming ceremony performed at the nearest station to the school after which the locomotive was named. No. 904 is seen in the up bay on one such occasion on 28th June 1930 in the company of the schoolboys of Lancing College. (H. M. Madgwick)

96. K class BR no. 32339 is seen from the footbridge, its smoke partly obscuring the goods yard and up bay. (E. Gamblin)

97. In 1893 the original station was extended rather than rebuilt. The style used was comple-
mentary but the materials were contrasting. This picture was taken in 1972, the year in which
BR planned to demolish these buildings and replace them with a standard modern station. Ten
years later they still stand virtually unaltered.   (J. Scrace)

98. The eastward view of the station in 1972 had changed little in the preceding eighty years.
Beyond the station there is a modern signal box with lifting barriers and colour light signals.
The gothic styled building is the parcels office. This view is unusual as the ornate windows are
normally obscured by poster boards (see photo 96) which had been removed during redecoration.
                                                                                    (J. Scrace)

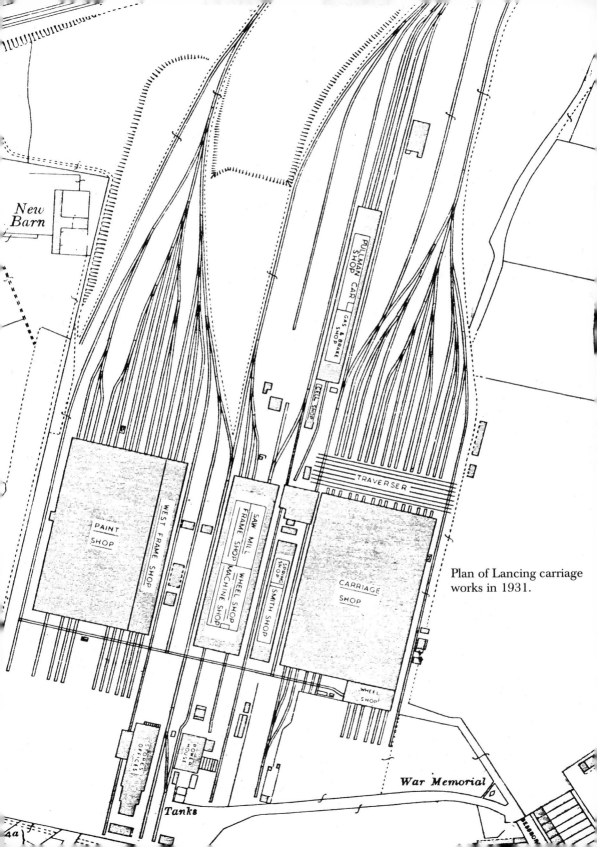

New Barn

PULLMAN SHOP CAR

GAS & BRAKE SHOP

CELL SHOP

PAINT SHOP

WEST FRAME SHOP

SAW MILL

FRAME SHOP

WHEEL SHOP

MACHINE SHOP

SIDING SHOP

SMITH SHOP

TRAVERSER

CARRIAGE SHOP

WHEEL SHOP

STORES OFFICES

POWER HOUSE

Tanks

War Memorial

Plan of Lancing carriage works in 1931.

LB&SC.R. Carriage Works, Lancing.

99. We cannot confirm the inscription on this photo as the details do not agree
with plans.
(C. Fry collection)

The following article by Dave Cox which appeared in the Bluebell News in 1974 is
reproduced by kind permission of the editor and gives an excellent idea of the work
involved in repairing a coach.

Upon arrival at Lancing the coach for heavy repair was examined from roof to rail level and briefly the sequence of events was as below. I have inserted the appropriate shop-roads and nicknames where the operation occurred. To the best of my knowledge the details are correct but it is now twelve years since I left Lancing so please forgive any errors.

Access between Carriage Shop Roads and Carriage Shop Yard was by Traverser, otherwise movements were all effected by locomotive, either 515S, 680S or an *E4*.

13 or 14 Road Carriage Shop Yard
Remove cells and dynamo for overhaul.
Wash Road
Wash interior paintwork.
Burn-off Road Carriage Shop
Burn off all exterior paint. Remove all interior polish with Nitro-Mors, neutralise and bleach.
Stripping Road Carriage Shop
Remove all trimming and brass/chrome/oxydised fittings for re-furbishing. All doors removed to Door-bay for repair.
Roofing Shed
Re-roof externally if required.
14 Road Carriage Shop
Replace bottom-side rails if necessary. (This entails the complete removal and replacement of the whole Body side). Special body repairs; i.e., after vehicle has been involved in a 'rough shunt'.
Pit Road Carriage Shop
Remove all brake rodding, shoes and hangers for re-bushing, etc. Fracture test draw and buffing gear.
High Road Carriage Shop
The coach body is lifted clear of the bogies by two 20-ton cranes and put on special high bogies. Until about 1955 the coaches moved down on a moving belt principle but subsequently the cranes performed the movements. Attention to brake cylinders, cell boxes, underneath wiring, the underframe, vacuum and steam mains, and draw and buffing gear. Whilst all this is happening 'up in the air', any special interior work; i.e., re-wiring and fitting of new ply-roof panels, is carried out. The first coat of white undercoat is applied to inside roof.

Meanwhile, the bogies are being boiled in caustic soda in a " Bosh tank ", then scraped clean and fitted with reconditioned springs from the Spring Shop and whatever new parts are necessary.

The wheels will have been turned, possibly fitted with new tyres and the axles tested with an ultra-sonic flaw detector.

The two whole bogies are then re-assembled and placed ready to receive the coach body at the end of the 'High Road'.
6 Road, Carriage Shop
Interior painting continues, also staining of surfaces to be polished. Lights (windows) removed and replaced with new putty and oiled felt (older stock) or rubbers (newer stock). Doors re-hung.
15 Road, Carriage Shop
Exterior panelling and mouldings repaired or replaced. All wiring to be completed in order that painters can complete their tasks on
13 Road, Carriage Shop
Exterior given two coats of grey primer, on top of red oxide.
Finishing Road, Carriage Shop
Seats replaced having been re-trimmed. Chrome/oxydised/brass fittings replaced and corridor doors rehung. The interior is now finished except for a final coat of clear varnish on polish work. This is done in the Paint Shop after transfers are applied.
Paint Shop
Exterior rubbed down, two coats of colour applied, the transfers and finally two coats of varnish. Between the rubbing down and the varnishing, the coach ends and roof would have been painted, new vestibule canvas fitted and brake rodding reinstated.
Cell Road
Overhauled cells and dynamo replaced. Steam heating tested.
Regulating Road
Primary and secondary suspension adjusted and buffer heights adjusted (on specially levelled road).
Paint Shop Yard
Brake test.
Stock Road or Klondike Siding
Coach ready for release to traffic.

During the time that the coach was in the works (ten weeks in the case of a 'Heavy') at least ten men would have been working on the coach or ancillary equipment, so that the number of man-hours was at least 3,000,

100. Class AI "Waddon" built in 1876 and numbered 54 was finally renumbered DS680 when it became Departmental Stock for shunting within the works. Locos no longer suitable for general traffic were used for this purpose. One problem with this old warrior when photographed in May 1958 was a defective front screw coupling. The fault was overcome by adding a 3-link wagon coupling. After withdrawal in 1965 it retired to Canada. (E. Wilmshurst)

	WEST WORTHING and BRIGHTON—(Motor Cars—One class only).—L. B. & S. C.																
Miles	Down.				Week Days.								Sundays.				
		mrn	mrn	mrn	aft	aft	aft	aft	aft	aft	aft	aft	mrn	mrn	mrn	aft	aft	aft	aft	aft	aft
	West Worthing....dep.		9 52		1 37	5 12				8	5 9	12										
½	Worthing ¶¶	7 8	9 55	11 35	1 41	5 15	4 40	6 15	7 35	8	8 9	15	1050	8 45	1010	1130	12 35	2 0	3 30	4 50	6 45	7 55
3	Lancing	7 14	10 1	11 41	1 46	5 21	4 46	6 21	7 41	8 14	9 21		1055	8 51	1016	1136	1241	2 6	3 36	4 56	6 51	8 1
5¼	Shoreham-by-Sea ¶	7 20	10 7	11 47	1 51	5 27	4 52	6 27	7 47	8 20	9 27		11 1	8 57	1022	1142	1247	2 12	3 42	5 2	6 57	8 7
6¼	Southwick ¶ ¶	7 24	10 11	11 51	1 55	5 31	4 56	6 31	7 51	8 24	9 31		11 5	9 1	1026	1146	1251	2 16	3 46	5 6	7 1	8 11
8¼	Portslade ¶ ¶	7 28	10 15	11 55	2 0	3 35	5 0	6 35	7 55	8 28	9 35		11 8	9 5	1030	1150	1255	2 20	3 50	5 10	7 5	8 15
9¾	Hove ¶¶ ....[195	7 32	10 19	11 59	2 6	3 39	5 4	6 39	7 59	8 32	9 39		1111	9 9	1034	1154	12 59	2 24	3 54	5 14	7 9	8 19
11¾	Brighton (C.) 180, arr.	7 38	10 25	12 5	2 12	3 45	5 10	6 45	8 5	8 38	9 45		1115	9 15	1040	12 0	1 5	2 30	4 0	5 20	7 15	8 25

‡ Station for Lancing College (2 miles).

¶¶ "Halts" at Ham Bridge, between Worthing and Lancing; Fishergate, between Southwick and Portslade; Dyke Junction, between Portslade and Hove ; and Holland Road, between Hove and Brighton.

☞ For OTHER TRAINS and Motor Cars between Brighton and Shoreham-by-Sea, see page 195.

∴ For OTHER TRAINS between West Worthing and Brighton, see pages 176 to 189.

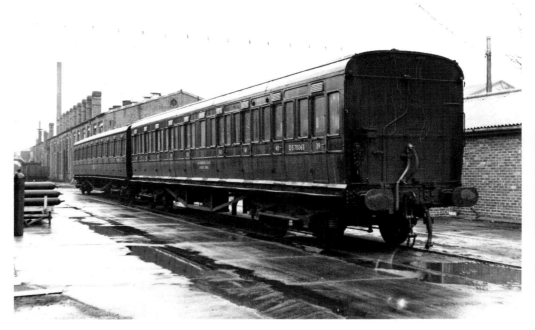

101. DS 70065 and DS 70063 formed part of the "Lancing Belle" and are seen here on a wet February day in 1964, near the end of their careers.   (E. Wilmshurst)

102. A rare interior view of the lofty carriage shop in March 1965 during the run-down before closure. It was taken from the south-west corner near road 15. The road numbers can be seen hanging from the roof trusses.   (E. Wilmshurst)

103.   The works sidings usually bore some unusual vehicles. In March 1965 they contained this rare petrol engined shunter DS 499 complete with outside mirrors (not for overtaking) and radiator muff, but minus couplings. It had been used for most of its life at the south end of the works transferring vehicles from 15 to 13 road.   (E. Wilmshurst)

104.   In the final years of the works one of its shunters was DS 236. This was one of a batch of locomotives built in the USA during World War II for service during the liberation of Europe and bought by the SR after the war.   (E. Wilmshurst)

EAST WORTHING HALT

This is one of the Motor trains halts opened in 1905. It was known as Ham Bridge until May 1949.

105. This view is included to emphasise the importance of horticultural traffic arising at the stations west of Hove. Special trains have been run regularly to the main markets, often overnight, with perishable glasshouse crops. (C. Fry collection)

106. This type of train working gave rise to the term push-pull, which continued to be used when the trains had shrunk so that the coaches were only on one side of the locomotive and were propelled by it in one direction. These coaches were introduced in 1912 for the coastal Motor Train services. (C. Fry collection)

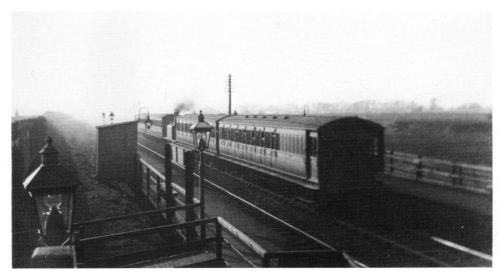

107.   Four train spotters look over the widened road bridge which was provided with new stairs to the platforms, both of which in the 1930's were still of timber construction.

(Lens of Sutton)

108.   A more recent view shows the platforms reconstructed in concrete and the stairs removed. The two profiles of the road bridge can be clearly seen.   (Lens of Sutton)

WORTHING

There have been three different stations on almost the same site. The first lasted until 1869, although the building still exists, and the second one was largely replaced in 1911. Between 1936 and 1968 it was known as Worthing Central.

109.   Looking towards Brighton at Worthing's first up platform, which was not opposite the down platform. Staggering of platforms was not uncommon in the early days of railways before the widespread use of footbridges and subways. This arrangement meant that passengers always crossed the line behind standing trains. The foot crossing is in the foreground.   (C. Fry collection)

110.   The exterior of the first station which was of brick and flint construction. It was later converted to a station master's house plus a cottage and the verandah was removed. It survives today having been the subject of a preservation order in 1971.   (C. Fry collection)

111.   The first and second stations stand together. Notice the old style signals and a windmill, the latter showing on the accompanying map of 1875. In 1881 it was moved to a more open site on the Lancing Road near Seamill Park Crescent.   (C. Fry collection)

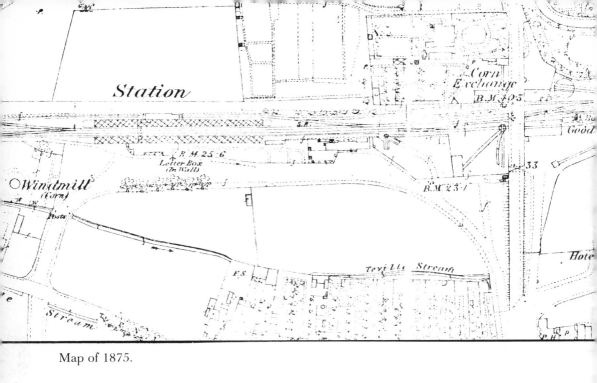

Map of 1875.

112. Looking eastwards at the vaulted canopies of the second station. Three gables of the canopy nearest the down starting signal and water crane were incorporated into the third station and still stand today.

(C. Fry collection)

113. The refreshment rooms were opened in 1879. This photograph was taken three years later and illustrates the fine tracery of the roof supports. The porter is about to demonstrate the carrying capacity of a sack truck.

(National Railway Museum)

114. Born in the year that the railway came to Worthing, Mr. A. T. Chapman was station master there from 1884 to 1907, having first served as booking clerk at Hailsham in 1860.

(H. C. P. Smail collection)

115.   Looking up Oxford Road around the turn of the century we see the rather unimpressive station dwarfed by the flamboyant style of the new Central Hotel. To the left of the station a wooden building was erected to serve as a sub-post office. This still exists, retained in the new building as a parcels office.   (C. Fry collection)

Map of 1898.   After reconstruction in 1908-11, two of the sidings were joined together to form the up loop and a third platform built alongside it. The introduction of motor trains made the turntable redundant, it being replaced by cattle docks.

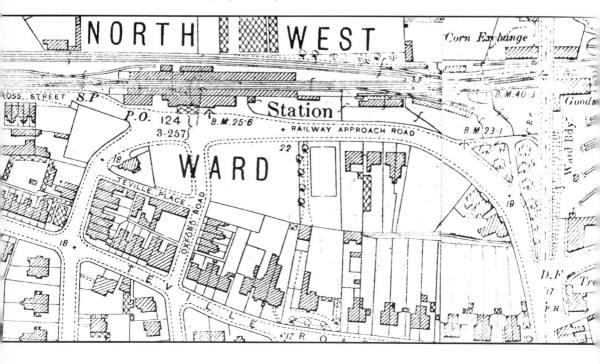

116. A contrast in travelling comfort was ready for passengers alighting from the LBSCR's new bogie coaches to continue their journey by road in this solid-tyred Milnes-Daimler. (C. Fry collection)

117. Worthing East Box (later 'A' box) and goods sheds, looking over the cattle dock in July 1924. All but the two LMS wagons still display the letters of the pre-grouping railway companies or private owners. (Late E. Wallis)

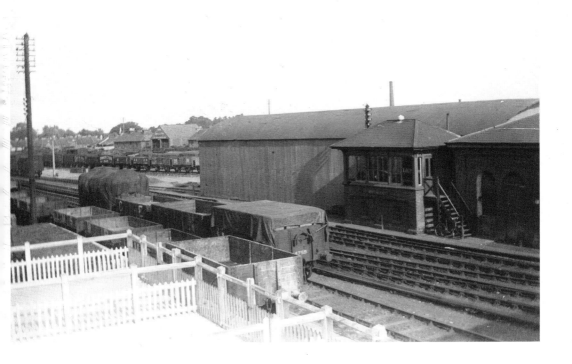

118.   In July 1936 Worthing was host to the Royal Counties Show and extra staff were brought in to assist in unloading the exhibits, such as the reaper and binder seen here in the air.

(G. Holmes collection)

119.   Portsmouth to Brighton train headed by class B4 no. 2051 pulling away with coaches of greatly differing ages. The electric down train is on its way to West Worthing, the limit of electri-fication at this time.   (H. M. Madgwick)

120.   Class I3 no. 2025 drifts under the Broadwater Road bridge past the end of the goods shed siding that had previously joined the down line here. The building on the left was the former corn exchange erected in 1852.   (C. Fry collection)

WEST SUSSEX RAILWAYS IN THE 1980s

This companion album by the same authors illustrates many of the changes that have taken place on the route since "Brighton to Worthing" was published. Mineral trains, charter specials and major engineering work add to the diversity of pictures, many of which are in colour. This update to 1990 is published by Middleton Press and adds another chapter to the long history of this interesting line.

121. Mr. H. H. Pelling was Worthing's station foreman from 1943 to 1952. When he retired after 46 years railway service he continued to live in the old station house.   (Worthing Gazette)

122.   Class E4 no. 32485 propels vans into the corrugated iron extension to the original goods shed in February 1957.   (P. Hay)

123.   Dieselisation eventually occurred. An O8 350 HP English Electric machine is seen at work here in 1969, the year before the yard was closed.   (J. A. M. Vaughan)

124.   Looking east, when the station was still "Central", at evidence of three stations. On the right, three gables of the second station attached to the long canopy of the present (third) station beyond which can be seen the chimneys of the first station.   (Lens of Sutton)

MP Middleton Press

Easebourne Lane, Midhurst, W Sussex. GU29 9AZ Tel: 01730 813169 Fax: 01730 812601
*If books are not available from your local transport stockist, order direct with cheque,
Visa or Mastercard, post free UK.*

BRANCH LINES
Branch Line to Allhallows
Branch Line to Alton
Branch Lines around Ascot
Branch Line to Ashburton
Branch Lines around Bodmin
Branch Line to Bude
Branch Lines around Canterbury
Branch Lines around Chard & Yeovil
Branch Line to Cheddar
Branch Lines around Cromer
Branch Lines of East London
Branch Lines to Effingham Junction
Branch Lines around Exmouth
Branch Line to Fairford
Branch Lines around Gosport
Branch Line to Hawkhurst
Branch Line to Hayling
Branch Lines around Horsham
Branch Lines around Huntingdon
Branch Line to Kingswear
Branch Lines to Launceston & Princetown
Branch Line to Longmoor
Branch Line to Looe
Branch Line to Lyme Regis
Branch Lines around March
Branch Lines around Midhurst
Branch Line to Minehead
Branch Lines to Moretonhampstead
Branch Lines to Newport (IOW)
Branch Line to Padstow
Branch Lines around Plymouth
Branch Lines to Seaton and Sidmouth
Branch Line to Selsey
Branch Lines around Sheerness
Branch Line to Shrewsbury
Branch Line to Swanage *updated*
Branch Line to Tenterden
Branch Lines to Torrington
Branch Lines to Tunbridge Wells
Branch Line to Upwell
Branch Lines around Weymouth
Branch Lines around Wimborne
Branch Lines around Wisbech

NARROW GAUGE BRANCH LINES
Branch Line to Lynton
Branch Lines around Portmadoc 1923-46
Branch Lines around Porthmadog 1954-94
Branch Line to Southwold
Two-Foot Gauge Survivors
Romneyrail
Vivarais Narrow Gauge

SOUTH COAST RAILWAYS
Ashford to Dover
Bournemouth to Weymouth
Brighton to Eastbourne
Brighton to Worthing
Chichester to Portsmouth
Dover to Ramsgate
Eastbourne to Hastings
Hastings to Ashford
Portsmouth to Southampton
Southampton to Bournemouth
Worthing to Chichester

SOUTHERN MAIN LINES
Basingstoke to Salisbury
Bromley South to Rochester
Crawley to Littlehampton
Dartford to Sittingbourne
East Croydon to Three Bridges
Epsom to Horsham

Exeter to Barnstaple
Exeter to Tavistock
Faversham to Dover
London Bridge to East Croydon
Orpington to Tonbridge
Tonbridge to Hastings
Salisbury to Yeovil
Swanley to Ashford
Tavistock to Plymouth
Victoria to East Croydon
Waterloo to Windsor
Waterloo to Woking
Woking to Portsmouth
Woking to Southampton
Yeovil to Exeter

EASTERN MAIN LINES
Fenchurch Street to Barking
Ipswich to Saxmundham
Liverpool Street to Ilford

WESTERN MAIN LINES
Ealing to Slough
Paddington to Ealing

COUNTRY RAILWAY ROUTES
Andover to Southampton
Bath Green Park to Bristol
Bath to Evercreech Junction
Bournemouth to Evercreech Jn.
Cheltenham to Andover
Croydon to East Grinstead
Didcot to Winchester
East Kent Light Railway
Fareham to Salisbury
Frome to Bristol
Guildford to Redhill
Porthmadog to Blaenau
Reading to Basingstoke
Reading to Guildford
Redhill to Ashford
Salisbury to Westbury
Stratford upon Avon to Cheltenham
Strood to Paddock Wood
Taunton to Barnstaple
Wenford Bridge to Fowey
Westbury to Bath
Woking to Alton
Yeovil to Dorchester

GREAT RAILWAY ERAS
Ashford from Steam to Eurostar
Clapham Junction 50 years of change
Festiniog in the Fifties
Festiniog in the Sixties
Isle of Wight Lines 50 years of change
Railways to Victory 1944-46
SECR Centenary album
Talyllyn 50 years of change
Yeovil 50 years of change

LONDON SUBURBAN RAILWAYS
Caterham and Tattenham Corner
Charing Cross to Dartford
Clapham Jn. to Beckenham Jn.
East London Line
Finsbury Park to Alexandra Palace
Kingston and Hounslow Loops
Lewisham to Dartford
Lines around Wimbledon
London Bridge to Addiscombe
Mitcham Junction Lines
North London Line
South London Line

West Croydon to Epsom
West London Line
Willesden Junction to Richmond
Wimbledon to Epsom

STEAMING THROUGH
Steaming through Cornwall
Steaming through Kent
Steaming through West Hants
Steaming through West Sussex

TRAMWAY CLASSICS
Aldgate & Stepney Tramways
Barnet & Finchley Tramways
Bath Tramways
Bournemouth & Poole Tramways
Brighton's Tramways
Camberwell & W.Norwood Tramways
Clapham & Streatham Tramways
Dover's Tramways
East Ham & West Ham Tramways
Edgware and Willesden Tramways
Eltham & Woolwich Tramways
Embankment & Waterloo Tramways
Enfield & Wood Green Tramways
Exeter & Taunton Tramways
Gosport & Horndean Tramways
Greenwich & Dartford Tramways
Hammersmith & Hounslow Tramways
Hampstead & Highgate Tramways
Hastings Tramways
Holborn & Finsbury Tramways
Ilford & Barking Tramways
Kingston & Wimbledon Tramways
Lewisham & Catford Tramways
Liverpool Tramways 1. Eastern Routes
Liverpool Tramways 2. Southern Routes
Maidstone & Chatham Tramways
North Kent Tramways
Norwich Tramways
Portsmouth's Tramways
Reading Tramways
Seaton & Eastbourne Tramways
Shepherds Bush & Uxbridge Tramways
Southampton Tramways
Southend-on-sea Tramways
Southwark & Deptford Tramways
Stamford Hill Tramways
Twickenham & Kingston Tramways
Victoria & Lambeth Tramways
Waltham Cross & Edmonton Tramways
Walthamstow & Leyton Tramways
Wandsworth & Battersea Tramways

TROLLEYBUS CLASSICS
Croydon Trolleybuses
Bournemouth Trolleybuses
Hastings Trolleybuses
Maidstone Trolleybuses
Reading Trolleybuses
Woolwich & Dartford Trolleybuses

WATERWAY ALBUMS
Kent and East Sussex Waterways
London to Portsmouth Waterway
West Sussex Waterways

MILITARY BOOKS
Battle over Portsmouth
Battle over Sussex 1940
Blitz over Sussex 1941-42
Bombers over Sussex 1943-45
Bognor at War
Military Defence of West Sussex
Secret Sussex Resistance
Sussex Home Guard

OTHER RAILWAY BOOKS
Garraway Father & Son
Index to all Middleton Press stations
Industrial Railways of the South-East
South Eastern & Chatham Railways
London Chatham & Dover Railway
War on the Line (SR 1939-45)